SCRUM BASICS

SCRUM BASICS

A VERY QUICK GUIDE TO AGILE PROJECT MANAGEMENT

TYCHO
PRESS

CONTENTS

INTRODUCTION

T he computer revolution began in California's Santa Clara Valley in the 1960s. William Shockley, one of the co-inventors of the transistor, had moved to the modest town of Mountain View there in 1956 to be closer to his ailing mother. He brought his company, Shockley Semiconductor, along with him. Among the first to work extensively in silicon transistors, Shockley attracted some of the best and brightest electronic engineers of the day to the area.

At Shockley and a variety of spin-offs and competitors, advances in transistor and integrated circuit technology drove the production of computers small enough (closet-sized) and fast enough (about one-thousandth as fast as the iPhone in your pocket today) that businesses could afford to use them to automate complex information-handling processes.

The trend accelerated quickly. In 1975, a Shockley Semiconductor alumnus named Gordon Moore, who had recently cofounded a scrappy semiconductor manufacturer called Intel, observed that the number of transistors that manufacturers could cram onto an integrated circuit roughly doubled every 18 months. With that, computing power would also roughly double.

The implications for business were clear: a new era of rapid information processing would lead to unheard-of efficiencies and productivity improvements. But by the 1980s, it was obvious that something was very wrong. Rather than skyrocket as computers entered the workforce, productivity rates flat-lined. Technology project failure rates exceeded 80 percent in the United States. Information technology (IT) hadn't delivered on the promise of increased efficiency, and no one seemed to know why.

Over time, it became evident that the problem lay not with the technologies themselves but with their implementation—no one had quite figured out how to use them efficiently yet. The business-management practices in vogue at the time had largely been established in the era of the assembly line, where careful planning, rigorous procedures, and step-by-step processes were lauded as keys to efficiency.

But this style of management proved wanting when it came to software development. Complexities arose that no one imagined in planning, procedures that non–software developers designed were ludicrous, and there was often dramatic miscommunication between stakeholders and developers.

In isolated pockets around the world, in businesses from IBM to Chrysler to small consulting firms no one had ever heard of, software developers were coming around to a different point of view. They believed that more flexible, adaptive methods of development were necessary to manage complex software projects. Independently, these developers began experimenting with new project-management techniques. Their separate trials led them to similar conclusions: rapid, short development cycles, improved communication between project participants, and increased adaptability in the face of changing requirements all resulted in more valuable software being produced more quickly than with traditional management models.

By the late 1990s, productivity gains finally started to surface. Agile development—which, when they finally got around to giving it a name, is what developers started to call the new model—has not been the only factor, but its impact in the world of software development has been undeniable.

And not just software development! Increasingly, agile methodologies are finding traction outside the IT world. Any complex development process, from building smartphones to creating marketing campaigns, can benefit from agile methods. For example, National Public Radio has started to use agile methods to develop new radio programs, and Wikispeed, a new auto company, uses it to build a car that can go 100 miles on a gallon of gas.

This book takes a closer look at one of the most popular of those agile frameworks, Scrum. Scrum is one of the oldest and most broadly used agile methodologies. You'll learn where Scrum came from, what makes it agile, and how to implement it. You'll see how to fill in the gaps that Scrum doesn't quite cover, and how the user community has adapted the framework to overcome common challenges. By the time you finish, you'll be out there scrumming with the best of them!

1 THE ESSENCE OF AGILE

The Agile Manifesto

We owe much of how we think about agile software development—including the term *agile* itself—to a handful of folks who got together at Snowbird, Utah, in 2001 to discuss alternative techniques to heavyweight "waterfall" development methods.

Some of these software developers, researchers, and consultants worked for big businesses, while others were independent. All were inveterate thinkers and tinkerers who recognized that existing development processes were dysfunctional. For example, they could spend months creating a program based on a set of detailed specs, only to find that some of the requirements had changed by the time they delivered the software. Or worse, early users would come back halfway through the development process and ask for elaborate changes that would blow project deadlines and budgets.

Each participant came to the same conclusion independently: elaborate, sequential software development didn't work, while sitting down and chatting with the people who actually used the software did work. Over time, developers adopted this kind of feedback loop and saw solid results. When they encountered one another at industry conferences or chatted on the Internet, it became clear that a trend was developing. The conference at Snowbird was orchestrated to discuss more fruitful development models in detail.

One of the conference attendees, Robert C. "Uncle Bob" Martin, worried that the nascent movement could fracture, sending software development back to the status quo of waterfall project management. So he showed up at Snowbird with an agenda: to get these developers to agree on a statement of purpose and principles for future software development.

The result is the Agile Manifesto, the disarmingly brief product of three days' worth of discussion among 17 thought leaders. It consists of seven sentences and fewer than 70 words, but the concepts it outlines changed the world of software development forever:

We are uncovering better ways of developing software by doing it and helping others do it. Through this work we have come to value:

- **Individuals and interactions** *over processes and tools*
- **Working software** *over comprehensive documentation*
- **Customer collaboration** *over contract negotiation*
- **Responding to change** *over following a plan*

That is, while there is value in the items on the right, we value the [bolded] items on the left more. (source: agilemanifesto.org)

Like Talmudic scholars, agile advocates may try to establish the exact balancing point of "over" in late-night Mountain Dew–fueled sessions, but the thrust of the values is cohesive and clear.

Agile Value 1: Individuals and Interactions over Processes and Tools

The jury is out—and may long be out—on whether programming is an expression of basic and replicable principles of software engineering or if it is a creative endeavor akin to artistic inspiration. Either way, the group at Snowbird agreed that an overemphasis on tools and blind adherence to process eclipsed the creative problem solving that took place when individuals communicated directly with one another.

No tool or process ever cranked out a worthwhile piece of software. Both the vision for a program and the code required to create it come from the human mind. When software creators become mired in a superfluous process rather than communicating directly, they're wasting effort and focus.

IBM hired one of the signers of the Agile Manifesto, Alistair Cockburn, in the early 1990s to design a methodology for object-oriented programming projects. Cockburn noted that the most successful teams he interviewed apologized for having no real methodology except sitting together and talking over problems. The least successful were puzzled by their failures; they had, after all, been using the most explicit, formal development processes they could find.

In general, agile methods use simple tools and a minimum of process. If you walk into a software company and see the walls covered with Post-It notes, odds are you're in an agile office. Post-Its aren't sexy, but they're functional. Most of the real success at agile companies results from interpersonal discussions, not wrestling with advanced project-management tools.

Agile Value 2: Working Software over Comprehensive Documentation

Agile developers minimize the effort they spend documenting software in favor of delivering the software itself. That's because the most fruitful discussions developers can have with clients is with a working product in front of them. No binder of requirements can substitute for a functioning model, even an incomplete one.

Detailed design documents take forever to develop yet almost always prove inadequate in the face of changing market conditions. Rather than wasting time on documentation, agile practitioners prioritize clean and functional code.

Not only does this emphasis on producing working software further the conversation between developers and customers, it engenders confidence between them. Agile practitioners can be sure they're meeting the customer's goals when the customer validates incremental progress. The customer, on the other hand, can see that the developer is building a valuable solution that meets their needs.

Agile Value 3: Customer Collaboration over Contract Negotiation

Customers may be internal or external, but the sole purpose of producing software is to offer them something of value. Developers must, of course, be compensated for providing that value. Yet detailed, up-front negotiations over the terms of what will and won't be produced run contrary to agile tenets, which demand flexibility and adaptability during development. That's because, at the beginning of a project, both developers and customers know too little about the project's pitfalls or efficiencies to accurately negotiate these details.

Ideally, developers and customers form a team. Clients almost always designate a customer proxy to provide as much feedback as possible. Either way, close collaboration between developer and client is a cornerstone of agile development.

This is right in line with Scrum's emphasis on the use of cross-functional teams. Agile methods seek to align the interests of developers and their clients, as well as efforts within the development team itself. By bringing project participants together on a self-directed team with broad discretion on how to implement the goals they are given, this technique brings a wider scope of information to the decision-making process. The collaborative process that results incorporates perspectives that may not receive sufficient attention in traditional development models.

Agile values hold that contracts are valuable when they enhance understanding and provide a foundation for collaboration. Agile methods seek to reduce risk to both developers and customers by delivering working products early and continuously.

Agile Value 4: Responding to Change over Following a Plan

The complex nature of software development and the fast pace of today's marketplace frequently foil elaborate up-front planning. Customers don't always know exactly what they want at the start of a project, and developers can't always be sure of what's possible until they attempt something.

Agile methods accept that the state of knowledge on both sides will improve as a project moves forward. Failing to use that new information to improve subsequent development efforts is madness, but traditional waterfall development doesn't allow for contingency changes like these—both developer and client are locked into the terms negotiated as part of the original plan.

There's tremendous value in avoiding decision lock-in early in the development process. Keeping options open until the last responsible moment lets developers provide more value to customers. The ability to go back to the customer and propose new solutions late in the game may greatly reduce the frustration of following plans that have become obsolete.

A New World

Taken together, these four simple precepts represent a strong rebuke of traditional waterfall software development. By extension, corporate traditionalists who accept the conventional industrial model of business organization and project management also see agile development as a threat.

That's because agile turns a lot of the conventional wisdom of business processes and scientific management on its head. The Industrial Age taught business managers that consistency, predictability, and specialization were the keys to profitability. An assembly-line model where each role could be exhaustively described in minute detail and whose workers could be trained and managed to conform to a standard resulted in quality products and efficient production.

Agile methodologies accept that consistency and predictability in software development is largely an illusion. Excessive specialization leads to information silos, which hide vital information from other individuals involved in the project. Centralized control by managers only results in unrealistic expectations and a breakdown in communication between software developers and customers.

Agile methods don't magically correct any of these basic project-management flaws. Software developers still need to talk to customers—if they don't, their initial plans will be flawed and impractical, and they'll overestimate their capabilities and underestimate implementation problems. Neither are managers instantly enlightened on what needs to be done; they still need to talk with developers and customers. And

A BRIEF HISTORY
OF AGILE DEVELOPMENT

The first 30 or 40 years of software development were marked by frustration on the part of both developers and the businesses they worked for. Software developers spent a lot of time developing code to specs that got tossed out the window before the project was finished, and businesses asked that programs automate certain tasks only to get a product that didn't work as expected.

Managers tended to stew and fire people when projects went off the rails, but developers tinkered. A few who were in a position to change the dynamics of software development did so.

Among those was a Smalltalk aficionado named Kent Beck. Chrysler hired Beck in 1996 to help develop a paycheck-processing system, which had stalled in development. Beck instituted a set of processes that became known as Extreme Programming (XP).

XP caught on with developers, and in 2000, Beck invited its adherents to Rogue River, Oregon, to discuss what were then known as "lightweight" development methods, XP being among them.

The meeting was a success, and two of the attendees, "Uncle Bob" Martin and Martin Fowler, thought a broader discussion with a wider range of lightweight developers would be beneficial.

They were instrumental in organizing the 2001 conference at Snowbird mentioned at the beginning of this section. There were 17 participants, including Beck, wiki inventor Ward Cunningham, and Scrum co-founders Ken Schwaber and Jeff Sutherland. Together, in the snow, they came up with 12 principles and a brief manifesto they could all agree on. And they decided on something to call it: agile.

agile projects still need processes, contracts, documentation, and plans.

Agile works a sort of project-management judo, dealing a cunning hip throw to these problems so they work in favor of creating a better product with fewer distractions.

None of this is to say that using agile methods is easy. If you're doing it right, you're probably putting a lot more effort into agile projects than you would be if you used traditional waterfall processes. It's not easy to constantly communicate with customers. It takes real discipline to self-organize and produce clean, working code on a regular schedule. Agile practitioners sleep well at night—they work for a living!

But they also sleep well because they don't waste effort. They don't fritter away months on features destined for the chopping block or on endless rounds of email tag. Instead, they accomplish goals, satisfy customers, and create value. What could be more fun?

Twelve Agile Principles

The Agile Manifesto has only four imperatives, but they're anchored in a set of 12 principles that the Manifesto's signatories believed should govern development.

1. Our highest priority is to satisfy the customer through early and continuous delivery of valuable software.

    Agile methods offer developers an unusual degree of freedom, but you shouldn't lose track of your ultimate

COMMON DIFFERENCES BETWEEN TRADITIONAL AND AGILE OFFICES

	TRADITIONAL OFFICE	AGILE OFFICE
Management	Top-down direction by professional managers.	Self-organizing teams of developers and customers.
Planning	Relies on theoretical, predictive planning models. Requirements are considered and researched, and imple-mentation plans are made well in advance of execution.	Uses empirical observation to plan in a constant cycle, relying on the most recent information and making commitments as they become necessary.
Failures	Belief that failure can be avoided with careful planning and rigorous adherence to established processes.	An acceptance of failure as part of the process, relying on rapid cycles to raise issues and allow quick corrections.
Process	Emphasizes previously established, predictable, replicable processes.	Focuses on results, analyzing and adapting processes throughout projects.

Continued ››

	TRADITIONAL OFFICE	AGILE OFFICE
Flexibility	Assumes that all variable factors in a project can be addressed in the planning phase, or addressed in a postproduction implementation.	Recognizes that uncertainty will emerge mid-project, and allows for adaptation to variables at any stage of development.
Documentation	Places considerable value in documentation. Documents are often considered the authoritative reference in the system.	Places more value in working software, minimizing documentation and maximizing interpersonal communication.
Decision-Making	Decisions are difficult to revisit once made. Decisions made by management flow down through layers, which insulate decision makers from consequences.	Pushes final decisions as late as possible, allowing changes to flow from observed reality. Decisions are left to the level closest to the systems affected.
Metrics	Progress is measured in comparison to the plan.	Progress is measured in terms of delivered, working software.

	TRADITIONAL OFFICE	AGILE OFFICE
Customers	Customers are consulted in the design and testing phases but rarely during development itself.	Customer interaction is stressed during all phases of development.
Quality Control	Errors or design flaws in a product are intended to be caught in a distinct testing phase, often by a separate testing team.	Emphasis is on quality code, ownership of results, and incremental completion, so errors are caught early in the process.
Responsibility	Responsibility is doled out individually to distinct roles, resulting in silos and turf wars.	Responsibility is handled collectively and shared across a team.
Authority	Authority is vested in managers or development leads, who retain the final say over almost every aspect of the development process.	Authority is distributed throughout the development team, each member of which is empowered to act within a framework to achieve project goals.
Morale	Employees walk the halls like zombies whose souls have been eroded in a merciless hail of bureaucracy.	Employees skip among cubicles like babes frolicking in idyllic meadows amid the first blossoms of spring.

objective of giving customers what they want. There's an easy and obvious way to do that: deliver the software they asked for.

2. Welcome changing requirements, even late in development. Agile processes harness change for the customer's competitive advantage.

   Agile processes give developers a lot of flexibility, but they demand flexibility *from* developers in return. Today's business marketplace moves quickly, and projects that can't adapt to change lose value quickly. If you're working on a cool new MP3 player and Fraunhofer suddenly decides to raise the codec licensing fee by 3,000 percent, you'd better get ready to switch to Ogg, or the project is toast.

   In complex processes like software development, customers can't always know what they want at the beginning of a project. Delivering rapid iterations of functional software helps them crystallize their requirements. You need to react to that feedback to deliver the best possible product in the next implementation.

3. Deliver working software frequently, from every couple of weeks to every couple of months, with a preference for the shorter time scale.

   If we haven't been clear enough on the topic so far, let's put it plainly here: working software is the coin of the agile realm. Delivering it frequently demonstrates your commitment to the customer and safeguards against risk, because the longer software stays in development without approval from your customer, the greater the risk of an invalid assumption being built into it. And those assumptions can be expensive if you leave them unchecked for long.

If a customer asks for a green color theme for their new website, it's better to find out early that they actually meant mint while you were thinking emerald. Otherwise, you might spend a lot of time undoing your own work late in the game.

4. Business people and developers must work together daily throughout a project.

   With a focus on customer satisfaction, agile development requires that you understand your customer sufficiently well to know what it takes to satisfy them. That happens only through regular interaction and feedback—you can get that unpleasant mint-versus-emerald misunderstanding out of the way with one quick conversation. And you'll find that the customer, if regularly consulted during development, will better understand the challenges and potential pitfalls of the project and have more opportunities to ensure that they'll get the product they want in the software.

5. Build projects around motivated individuals. Give them the environment and support they need, and trust them to get the job done.

   Agile methods demand much of developers, but they also offer a considerable amount of independence, too much for many traditional managers. A constant source of friction in offices that adopt agile techniques comes from managers who just can't understand how anything can get done if they don't personally oversee each step of the process.

The solution is to hire a motivated staff, give them what they need, and trust them to deliver. The manager's role in agile offices shifts from one of supervision to one of service. Managers should step in only to exercise their managerial powers to dispatch obstacles confronting the team.

6. The most efficient and effective method of conveying information to and within a development team is face-to-face conversation.

Agile proponents recognize that humanity has yet to invent a way to communicate that 100,000 years of evolution can't beat. Texting, social media, email—none of these incorporate all of the efficiency and subtlety afforded by simply talking directly with another human being. Today's technologies are excellent supplements to direct communication, but tone, body language, and a hundred other subtle expressions make all these tools less effective than a quick chat over coffee.

Most agile methodologies implement a way to meet this requirement in a practice called the Daily Scrum, which forces Scrum teams to spend *at least* 15 minutes each day speaking to one another.

7. Working software is the primary measure of progress.

Traditional development methodologies offer management a lot of progress metrics: milestones, reviews, sign-offs, lines of code written, hours worked. But it turns out that almost none of them correlate to successful product delivery. So what does? Actually delivering working software.

Regularly producing working software is one of the factors that lets managers trust developers with a high degree of freedom.

8. Agile processes promote sustainable development. The sponsors, developers, and users should be able to maintain a constant pace of development indefinitely.

Traditional software development frequently results in a so-called death march as release dates approach, unfinished features run afoul of uncovered bugs, and every developer works 16 hours a day to avoid slipping.

Because agile processes call for short iterations, there's a risk that teams will slide into a constant death march mode, always hustling to hit that upcoming cycle date.

To counter this, teams should pace themselves and avoid taking on more work than they can sustainably accomplish in any given iteration. Short iterations are easier to sell to customers, too—if you can't finish a feature this month, you can have it ready for next month. By having a lot of deadlines, you avoid the one big make-or-break moment at the end of a development cycle.

9. Continuous attention to technical excellence and good design enhances agility.

From a technical perspective, much of agile development revolves around not coding yourself into a corner. Rapid feedback cycles reduce this risk, but good coding practices are essential.

By programming at a deliberate, sustainable pace and focusing on solid design and clean code, you reduce your technical debt and give yourself room to handle shifting requirements.

10. Simplicity—the art of maximizing the amount of work not done—is essential.

    It's always tempting to try to get ahead of the game. What's more satisfying than moving on to your next task, knowing that you foresaw what was necessary and already wrote most of the code the week before?

    But this is also a trap. If it were so easy to foresee requirements, waterfall methods would work perfectly well for software development. In reality, trying to predict what you need usually results in building a never-used feature or one that you have to redo as you learn more about the objective.

    Agile development dodges this bullet by focusing on the bare minimum required to accomplish the goal that's best understood and most immediately necessary to add value to the product.

11. The best architectures, requirements, and designs emerge from self-organizing teams.

Rather than rely on upper management to produce requirements and product designs, agile methods push these activities down to the lowest possible level. This ensures that the people most familiar with the project's day-to-day requirements and obstacles make the tactical decisions. The customer still provides strategic direction for the product, but the agile team itself decides how to build it, relying on its own expertise.

12. At regular intervals, the team considers how to become more effective, and then tunes and adjusts its behavior accordingly.

The way a self-organizing team self-organizes is a matter of practice and effort. The feedback loops in agile development go beyond the product being produced. Agile teams also look at and continuously adjust their own processes for better efficiency. Scrum, for example, reviews team performance independently of product development, which helps uncover any systemic problems in development.

Popular Agile Frameworks

Agile sprang from a dozen seeds, and each sapling grew into a slightly different tree.

When "Uncle Bob" Martin et al. wrote the Agile Manifesto in 2001, software developers and their managers knew there were more practical and better alternatives to waterfall development. Software developers used iterative development in various projects, and those early experiments led to more formalized development frameworks.

Aficionados developed few, if any, agile frameworks in a purely theoretical environment. They spontaneously established most in response to floundering real-world software projects or those that represented an overwhelming challenge using traditional heavyweight development methods. Consequently, each agile framework represents a slightly different take on agile methods, shaped by the reality of a project or the company that deployed it.

Although all agile frameworks embrace the 12 agile principles in one form or another, their emphasis or degree of commitment may differ. Some prescribe certain definite technical practices for software developers to follow, while others have little to say about specific techniques in favor of more general process oversight.

What follow are seven of the most popular agile development methodologies and their differences.

> In *The Mythical Man-Month*, Fred Brooks explored the pitfalls of conventional assumptions about productivity when applied to software projects, based on his experiences on the IBM OS/360 project. His tenet, which has become known as Brooks's Law, was that "adding manpower to a late software project makes it later."

Lean Software Development

Lean development evolved from the lean manufacturing methods (a collection of tactical methods designed to eliminate waste and improve efficiency in manufacturing environments) that helped inspire agile software development. Lean embraces many of the same terms and principles as the Toyota Production System, the precursor to all lean manufacturing systems.

Lean isn't a specific method or framework. Instead, it complements existing business practices with a set of principles that emphasize return on investment and improved business metrics.

Lean focuses on eliminating wasted effort by following these seven principles:

- Eliminate waste
- Amplify learning
- Decide as late as possible
- Deliver as fast as possible
- Empower the team
- Build quality in
- See the whole

You most often find lean software development in manufacturing, where it dovetails neatly with lean manufacturing practices, and in startups focused on rapid prototyping and market testing.

THE MVP, OR MINIMUM VIABLE PRODUCT

Agile methodologies tend to support another recent and popular trend, that of lean startup companies oriented toward producing a Minimum Viable Product (MVP) for piloting products to market.

The idea behind an MVP is agile to the core: to quote Eric Ries, one of the initial proponents of the concept and author of *The Lean Startup*, a book popularizing the term, "The minimum viable product is that version of a new product which allows a team to collect the maximum amount of validated learning about customers with the least effort."

The lean startup concept extends this idea to the organization producing the MVP: it may consist of no more than the minimum necessary staff and systems required to produce that minimal product in the first place.

This all fits in neatly with the agile principle of simplicity, "maximizing the amount of work not done."

In the same way that a potentially shippable product increment is designed to validate client expectations by presenting working software for their feedback, an MVP can collect similar data from customers in the wild. By doing so with a minimum of development investment, bad product ideas are discarded swiftly and good ones funded rapidly.

An MVP is often not a product at all in the traditional sense of the word. It may be as minimal as an ad for a product that doesn't yet exist, or a website that offers a service which has not yet been built.

Because the MVP is primarily about learning and adjusting to the market, it is a natural fit for the Scrum mantra of "inspect and adapt."

Kanban

Kanban is less a software development framework than a way to enhance visualization and workflow in just-in-time production systems. You may find it used hand in hand with other frameworks. Many Scrum teams, for example, use Kanban to manage their product backlog and work-in-process items (called Scrumban).

You can use Kanban as a complementary method in any existing development or production process, not just with other agile methods. In fact, Kanban was originally developed as an integral part of the Toyota Production System and sees its heaviest adoption in lean manufacturing companies.

One of Kanban's tenets is to respect the processes, roles, and titles that exist in the organizations that adopt it. This makes it an excellent choice for companies that have considerable internal resistance to adopting agile processes wholesale. Kanban can provide greater transparency into current processes and a small taste of the advantages of agile without disrupting your staff.

A Kanban variant called Open Kanban has been introduced as a development method specifically designed for software development. It embraces the following practices:

- Visualize the workflow
- Lead using a team approach
- Reduce the batch size of your effort
- Learn and improve continuously

Extreme Programming (XP)

XP is one of the earliest agile software development methodologies. It has both inspired the movement and drawn detractors for its unusual programming practices. Unlike many other agile methods, XP lays out explicit technical practices and demands rigorous adherence to those specifications.

You can imagine XP as agile to the max. XP's rules are simple, but there are a lot of them, and many practitioners find it difficult to comply.

XP has been controversial both because it was among the first detailed agile methodologies and because of its insistence on rigid conformance to programming practices that were, at the time they were introduced, rather unusual.

Yet in the years since, many of XP's technical practices have found their way into the mainstream. You'll find them popularized today as a part of other agile methodologies, although often applied with less rigor.

At heart, XP recognizes four basic activities for developers:

- Coding
- Testing
- Listening
- Designing

The framework assumes that every developer performs each of these tasks daily.

Unique among the agile pantheon, XP calls for "courage" on the part of developers, surely a useful quality for any new agile practitioner.

"Pure" XP isn't often seen in the wild these days, but its influence on every other agile methodology is hard to understate.

Crystal Methods

The Crystal Methods are a complete family of agile methodologies. They're color-coded (e.g., Clear, Yellow, Red, Orange, and so on) and differentiated by their applicability to projects of a given size.

The framework differs from most other agile methodologies in explicitly acknowledging "safety" as a consideration in the development process. Crystal recognizes that some software projects have a lower tolerance for failure than others.

Uniquely, the roles and artifacts each Crystal variation uses scale according to the size and criticality of the project. Depending on the formality of the method selected, Crystal can have an unusually large number of roles compared to other agile methodologies.

This lets you apply Crystal Methods to projects that aren't seen as good candidates for other agile frameworks. The agile mantra of "embrace failure" sounds a little less compelling when you're discussing heart monitors or nuclear power plant control systems. Even many agile practitioners acknowledge a role for the rigors of waterfall models in such cases. But the Crystal Methods offer a slowly escalating degree of formality and process that can provide many of the safeguards offered by sequential development models without abandoning agile principles.

Other than a few niches, however, the Crystal Methods never really caught on in the agile universe (quite possibly because the framework had the misfortune of being introduced around the time that the band of the same name was skyrocketing in popularity—Google searches for the term led to music, not methods). The family exists largely as a theoretical construct exploring a number of ideas for agile methodologies that may still be ahead of their time.

Dynamic Systems Development Method (DSDM)

DSDM emerged from the business world rather than the programming world. Consequently, it focuses on business concerns, like budgets and timeliness, that other agile methods de-emphasize.

In fact, budget and timing are central to DSDM. The method calls for a fixed budget and time frame for a project, and then

> Ironically, DSDM's two-pass model borrows a key, and often overlooked, component from the first formalized description of the waterfall methodology. In his 1970 article "Managing the Development of Large Software Systems," Winston Royce incorporated the idea that the software version delivered to a customer should be the second version written, the first serving as a prototype from which to learn.

uses rapid prototyping and iterative development to scale down functionality to match the available schedule and resources.

DSDM doesn't mandate programming practices, and it includes a phase model that superficially resembles some sequential development practices. The phases in the model are:

- Feasibility/business study
- Functional model iteration
- Design/build iteration
- Implementation

Unlike other agile methods, DSDM separates the initial modeling work from the final implementation work.

DSDM was invented in England and remains more popular in India and Europe than in the United States. A not-for-profit corporation, the DSDM Consortium, maintains the official standards for the framework.

Feature-Driven Development (FDD)

FDD may be unique in the agile world in that it was initially created to work with large development teams. Most other agile methods specify team sizes of between 7 and 12 people, but FDD started with 50.

Like XP, FDD has a number of things to say about programming practices. FDD calls for individual "ownership" of code classes, code inspections, configuration management, and a regular build process. It revolves around a feature list developed to fit a high-level model of the software. You assign teams the features they should implement rather than having all the members work on the same feature at once. This technique is part of what makes FDD attractive for larger projects—you can add teams as necessary to speed up development.

FDD involves five steps:

1. Develop an overall model
2. Build a features list
3. Plan by feature
4. Design by feature
5. Build by feature

FDD wasn't intended to cover the entire software development process, only the design and build phases. Delivery and customer feedback aren't explicit components of the model.

Scrum

Scrum emphasizes a team-based, collaborative development approach organized around an ongoing series of short "sprints" that produce incremental and releasable versions of the software.

Scrum may be the most popular agile framework in use today. It includes a very limited number of roles and activities, even in comparison to other agile methodologies; its implementation is straightforward; and it offers a strong community and well-developed certification program. Scrum also avoids mandating specific programming practices, allowing development teams to find their own comfort level with tools and techniques.

Scrum consists of three roles, three artifacts, and five activities:

ROLES

- Product owner
- Scrum master
- Development team member

ARTIFACTS

- Product backlog
- Sprint backlog
- Potentially shippable product increment (PSPI)

ACTIVITIES

- Product backlog grooming
- Sprint planning
- Daily Scrum
- Sprint review
- Sprint retrospective

The lack of specificity at the task level makes Scrum uniquely suited to projects apart from software development. In recent years, it has made inroads as a general project-management framework. Scrum also has support in the form of the Scrum Alliance, a nonprofit organization that manages a formal certification process for each of the respective roles.

WATERFALL VERSUS AGILE: GET READY TO RUMBLE!

The debate over waterfall versus agile product development is not new and shows no signs of dying anytime soon. The Agile Manifesto was expressly written as a critique of the then-prevalent waterfall development model, and it was inevitable that waterfall fans would take it poorly. Comparisons between them have evolved into a sort of online blood-sport for industry pundits.

This book is about one of the flagship frameworks for agile development and comes down squarely in the agile camp. But waterfall development is not without strengths, and agile is not beyond all criticism.

Agile detractors frequently level the charge that agile simply slaps a set of new and amorphous terms on long-standing concepts from the waterfall development world and then speeds up the whole obfuscated process to the point where no one understands it. Even some of the signatories of the manifesto feel that, in practice, agile has devolved into a meaningless collection of buzzwords.

Both agile and waterfall are vulnerable to certain systemic problems. Agile often fails in rigid environments or when practiced by neophytes. Waterfall does poorly when requirements aren't precisely defined or where capabilities are not well understood.

Most of the critiques leveled against either approach, then, tend to revolve around scenarios where they were selected inappropriately for the project. The fact is that small, risky projects tend to make agile approaches look good while large, predictable projects fit well in the waterfall model.

Now, can't we all just get along?

2 SPOTLIGHT ON SCRUM

Introducing Scrum

Scrum is one of the oldest formal agile methodologies around. It emerged in the mid-1990s as a set of practices derived from the scholarly paper "The New New Product Development Game," published in the *Harvard Business Review* in 1986.

The two men most closely associated with the origin of Scrum, Ken Schwaber and Jeff Sutherland, independently established similar programming practices for projects in the early 1990s. Comparing notes, they realized they were implementing the same principles, and they co-presented a paper on Scrum methodology in 1995.

Since then, Scrum has become one of the most widely used agile frameworks. According to market analyst Forrester Research, more than 90 percent of organizations that identify as "agile" use Scrum as their methodology. Scrum is used in all kinds of environments, from small projects with a handful of participants to major projects that coordinate the work of hundreds of people producing some of the most well known and widely used software on the planet today.

The lore of the framework now caroms around the Internet and through coffee shops and high-tech workplaces. The uninitiated puzzle at talk of pigs and chickens, sprints, spikes, velocity, and ScrumBut. They wonder how you win at a hand of Planning Poker and if a Scrumban will get you thrown out of the office.

It's true that Scrum has a lot of titles, games, and funny activities associated with it, but these are just labels. The core of the Scrum method is built around agile principles and the values behind them. Developers use the framework as an aid in creating and rapidly delivering valuable, working software to customers.

Three Roles

Scrum uses only a few titles. There are no team leads, project managers, or chief designers. Team members handle multiple tasks that don't reflect the territoriality that such titles tend to foster. So there are only three formal roles in the framework, described as follows.

Product Owner

Scrum calls for a single person in the role of product owner. He is ultimately responsible for realizing the value of a product based on the work put into it. He accomplishes this by prioritizing items in the product backlog and determining the acceptance criteria for items to be marked done.

No one other than the product owner can perform these actions, and no one else in the organization can make direct requests of the development team. The product owner is the single point of contact for external stakeholders seeking new features or changes to the product.

For Scrum to work, managers have to recognize the product owner as the product backlog's ultimate gatekeeper. Executives who regularly circumvent owners quickly erode the owner's effectiveness, and teams that don't respect the owner's authority often find themselves pulled in different directions by competing requests.

That authority comes with heavy responsibility, however. The owner must incorporate the wishes and needs of external stakeholders into the overall vision for the product, and ensure that the development team understands those wishes.

In addition, the product owner serves as the customer's representative to the team and participates in various team activities to provide that perspective. They also act as a resource for team members who require clarification or additional information on requirements. Any time developers have to wait for an answer about a feature they're working on is time wasted. Product owners have to be constantly available to resolve these questions.

In general, product owners:

- Own the product backlog and prioritize items
- Act as the definitive interface between external stakeholders and the rest of the Scrum team
- Make the final judgment on whether a product is a potentially shippable product increment

Development Team

Unlike the way Scrum limits the product owner role to a single person, it doesn't limit the size of the development team. According to official lore, the team should be "small enough to remain nimble and large enough to complete significant work within a sprint."

People usually interpret this as meaning that teams should include between five and nine members. The number should be small enough to foster excellent communication while large enough to include people with enough technical expertise to produce a potentially shippable product increment without outside assistance.

The exact composition of the team depends on the product you're developing. Some teams are composed exclusively of software developers. Others might have a mixture of software developers, artists, and quality-assurance specialists.

Regardless of team members' specialties, Scrum practitioners expect everyone to pitch in and help with whatever task has priority. Development teams can't afford passengers during a sprint—everyone needs to work. If that means an artist ends up doing some testing, or a tester chips in with some simple programming, that's how it goes. The upside is that every team member learns a little bit about every role required to complete a project.

Beyond their day-to-day responsibilities, members of the development team also have to be managers. Scrum teams are self-organizing, although Scrum doesn't dictate how teams should structure themselves. Rather, every team should find its own dynamic for collaborating on important chores like estimating, task breakdown, and work assignments. If you previously spent a lot of time sitting at your desk thinking about how easy your manager's job is, you'll lose that attitude after a few days on a Scrum development team. Managing is hard work, and teams that do well take it seriously.

The development team is a unified force. The members live and die together. They share successes and failures. They don't allow for blame or finger-pointing. In short, their goals are to:

- Create item estimates
- Self-organize
- Complete product backlog items to agreed-upon standards

Scrum Master

One of the things that most differentiates Scrum from other agile frameworks is the role of Scrum master. Every other framework has an analog for the product owner, and all of them include developers, but none incorporates a role so unique as that of Scrum master.

This is in part because Scrum methods try to improve processes not just for the product you're developing but for the process of development itself. The Scrum master doesn't owe allegiance to the product owner, and he's not a member of the development team. Instead, his devotion is to the process. He makes Scrum shops run smoothly.

Because of this, it's hard to precisely define the Scrum master's role. You hear the word *coach* thrown around a lot, and it's true that coaching is part of the job. But Scrum masters should also operate in the ill-defined space where unexpected problems may occur. They're general troubleshooters, seeking out and working to eliminate obstacles that prevent a team from producing valuable software.

Those problems might be internal. The team might have difficulty communicating or keeping the Daily Scrum on schedule, for example. In such cases, the Scrum master should step in and help resolve those issues.

But obstacles can be external, too: outside stakeholders might bypass the product owner to make requests of the development team, or the team might need external resources they can't procure. The Scrum master takes action in these situations, too.

You might hear "pigs" and "chickens" every once in a while when people talk about Scrum teams. These aren't formal roles. They refer to an old joke about a pig and a chicken talking about opening a restaurant together called "Ham and Eggs." The pig backs out, saying, "You'd be involved, but I'd be committed!" The idea is that only "pigs" should have the final say in decisions they commit to, and "chickens " should listen quietly.

The Scrum masters are masters in the Zen sense; no one owes them obeisance, and they have no special authority over the development team. They might not even have a programming background. Instead, Scrum masters exercise leadership by example. They epitomize the Scrum process, serving as a resource for addressing unexpected problems and applying specialized Scrum judo moves to circumvent unforeseen obstacles.

The Scrum master is a resource for both the product owner and the development team. If conflicts or communication problems arise between them, he resolves them. He helps the business adapt to agile principles and coaches the team to live up to them. Among the master's duties are to be

- well versed in agile principles and a Scrum expert,
- responsible for helping the team improve at Scrum, and
- responsible for facilitating communication among the team and with external stakeholders.

Scrum Activities and Artifacts

One thing that makes Scrum so popular is its adaptability. It's flexible enough for a variety of development projects. One factor that makes it so effective is its discipline on the development process. Flexibility without some stabilizing force is chaos. Like a bamboo trellis, Scrum bends to accommodate unexpected breezes, but it remains strong and keeps the team in alignment through even the heaviest storm.

Scrum has relatively few artifacts and activities, but they're the bamboo rods that hold the framework together; you can't discard them without serious consequences.

The mechanics of Scrum are a series of short loops revolving around a small number of prescribed artifacts and activities. The core framework describes a minimum number of these. Many teams add others to deal with specific situations or preferences. There's nothing wrong with that! The Scrum mantra is "inspect and adapt."

As you'll see, Scrum seeks continuous improvement not just in the product but in the Scrum process itself. Just keep the various principles of agility in mind as you tweak things, and you'll be fine.

Each activity has specific participants and a particular duration. The duration is pegged to the time frame your team selects for the sprint itself. You'll find them listed as fractions of a hypothetical one-month sprint; you should scale them as appropriate for your sprint duration.

> ScrumBut describes Scrum implementations that, well, aren't really Scrum. The phrase comes from practitioners describing their method as, "We use Scrum, but . . ." and then going on to describe how they really aren't using Scrum at all.

Grooming

Duration: Unspecified; often set to 10 percent of sprint duration

Participants: Product owner, development team

The product owner works with stakeholders to create the items that populate the product backlog. The owner sets the value and priority of each item. The members of the development team, on the other hand, exclusively determine the resource estimates for those items.

To populate, value, and describe list items, the product owner and development team collaborate in an activity called grooming, or story time. Although the owner has the final say over the user story, value, and priority, he relies on feedback from the development team to break items into sprint-appropriate chunks. Similarly, as the development team estimates items, the product owner provides detail and a better understanding of the customer perspective, which can make those estimates more accurate.

Grooming is an ongoing process. You can't know all the items required for a project at its beginning because that

> You may represent the numbers assigned to estimates and values in different units of measure, including hours or dollars. But since most teams use the values as a relative sense of a task's requirements, they often use imaginary "story points" as values to avoid confusion.

PRODUCT BACKLOG

The product backlog is the Scrum artifact around which all the efforts of the Scrum team revolve. It consists of an array of prioritized items that, collectively, describe the product's features.

Product backlog items should have the following attributes:

- **Description.** A summary of the item, usually presented in the form "As a [type of user], I want to [do something] in order to [accomplish some goal]."

- **Order.** The relative priority an item has versus other items in the list.

- **Estimate.** The development team's estimate of how much work is required to build an item. It can't be longer than the time available in a single sprint.

- **Value.** The business value the item represents. Normally, but not always, this corresponds to the item's order.

Scrum teams sometimes call items "user stories" because they typically describe in plain-English terms a function that a customer wants based on the user perspective. To encourage brevity, teams often write items on 3x5 cards or sticky notes—a story that won't fit on a card is probably not singular and discrete enough to represent a single item.

Teams don't resolve all the items to the same level of detail at the same time. High-priority items, which the team will finish first, will be smaller and better understood. Low-priority items will be broken down, refined, and estimated as they move up the list in the grooming process.

can change as new information and the results of previous iterations come in. In fact, planning for the unknown is antithetical to agile principles.

Scrum doesn't dictate a set time in the sprint for grooming. Many teams groom during weekly meetings.

Sprint Planning

Duration: 8 hours
Participants: Full Scrum team

When you plan a sprint, you move product backlog items to the sprint backlog so your team can figure out what they need to do to complete the items. This is usually facilitated by breaking the meeting into two phases: the first to prioritize items, and the second to identify item tasks.

PRIORITIZING ITEMS

When you finish grooming, you should have a list of prioritized, detailed, and estimated items at the top of the product backlog stack. The product owner presents this list to the development team as candidates for inclusion in the sprint

There's some debate in the Scrum world over describing the inclusion of items in the sprint backlog. The original Scrum descriptions use the word *commitment*; some practitioners prefer the word *forecast*.

backlog. The group then reviews the user story to the satisfaction of all parties and agrees on acceptance criteria for the items.

Then the development team decides whether it can commit to delivering that item during the current sprint. Crucially, the product owner has no say in this decision. The software developers who actually do the work make the decision.

You repeat this process until the development team adds as many items as it believes it can deliver. Then you move on to the next phase.

IDENTIFYING TASKS

The team then breaks the accepted items down into tasks required to complete them. The entire team must agree on the definition of done. The development team will probably discuss this in some detail, and it may consult the product owner for clarification.

As it does with the backlog items themselves, the development team often estimates how much work each task will

The definition of done comes up frequently in Scrum. It may vary from team to team, but it must be consistent within the team itself. Since the sprint will result in a potentially shippable product increment, your definition has to include every bit of work required to get the product increment to a customer.

SPRINT BACKLOG

A sprint backlog consists of items selected from the product backlog by mutual consent of the product owner and development team for completion during the next sprint.

The owner and development team flesh out the items with associated tasks, often creating a detailed acceptance test for the item so both parties know what functionality constitutes done for that item.

The team creates the sprint backlog during sprint planning. Once a team adds an item to the backlog, the product owner can't change the item mid-sprint. Nor is he allowed to add items during the sprint.

The development team, on the other hand, is free to consult with the product owner to request changes to items as they work on and learn more about the challenges of implementing the items. They track their progress as they proceed, and add tasks they may find necessary later in the sprint. Or, if they find other tasks taking less effort than imagined, they can ask for additional items to be added to the sprint backlog during the sprint.

Anyone can request that an item be dropped from the sprint entirely. For example, the product owner may realize that business or market changes have rendered an item obsolete, or the development team may realize they can't deliver for technical reasons on that particular sprint.

require. That helps it apportion the tasks internally, though that doesn't need to happen during the planning meeting. In any case, no one outside the development team can assign tasks or create breakdowns.

Occasionally, an estimate might be overly optimistic. If that happens, the development team and product owner reexamine the sprint backlog and drop or shuffle items to fit the available "capacity." How is that capacity determined? For the first few iterations of a product cycle, it may involve a series of WAGs (wild-ass guesses) based on individual experience. Once the team has a few sprints under its belt, it will have enough experience to know how much it can accomplish during an average sprint—which it can then use to estimate capacity for future sprint planning sessions.

Sprints

Duration: 1 month maximum; fixed value
Participants: Development team

Sprint execution is the meat in the Scrum sandwich. All of a project's coding takes place during a sprint. You schedule sprints back to back, and activities like planning and grooming take place as part of them (see figure 1 on page 58).

Sprints may not last longer than a calendar month. While this may appear to be a limitation, it's actually one of Scrum's great enabling tenets. Here's why:

- A sprint's scope is inherently restricted, so it doesn't allow for pie-in-the-sky items.

- It lets the development team reasonably reject meddling and additions in the middle of a job.
- At the same time, it provides the product owner with frequent opportunities to adjust the project trajectory at the next iteration.
- The risk of poor development decisions is limited; the maximum amount of work that can be wasted is the length of the sprint.
- Business value is created at the end of each cycle.

The Daily Scrum

Duration: 15 minutes maximum
Participants: Development team

Every day during a sprint, the development team meets briefly to coordinate (Self-organizing, remember? What, did you think that happened by magic?) and answer three quick questions:

- What did you do yesterday?
- What will you do today?
- Are there any obstacles preventing you or others on the team from accomplishing that goal?

To encourage focus and brevity, teams often conduct this meeting standing up—don't get too comfortable, just spit it out and move on. The Scrum master may enforce the time limit and the limits on participation.

Although only development team members participate in the Daily Scrum, many teams let the product owner or other

POTENTIALLY SHIPPABLE PRODUCT INCREMENT

The potentially shippable product increment (PSPI) might be the single most confusing concept in Scrum. Its intent is clear enough: in accordance with agile principles, the primary metric by which you should measure all progress is working software that performs functions of value to the customer and is delivered frequently.

But then things start to get foggy. What, exactly, does *working* mean? What makes a function valuable? Is the product really shippable if the first sprint delivered only 5 percent of the required features?

PSPI is a hedge against all these questions. Like other Scrum labels, it's valuable less for the term itself than as a placeholder for a mutually agreed-on definition. You should read *potentially shippable* as a statement on the quality of the code increment:

- It should be fully tested.

- It should be clean and refactored.

- It should be done according to the team definition.

Because you're working in brief, iterative cycles, no one expects a product to be finished at the end of the first iteration. Yet the goal for each sprint is to maximize the potential for the incremental result to be released as a valuable product by itself. If the project were cancelled at that moment, the business should still have a working piece of software with some genuine value.

stakeholders attend and observe. This improves the transparency of the sprint process, which is relatively opaque to the outside world.

Of course, issues may be raised during the Daily Scrum that the team can't resolve in 15 minutes. But resolution isn't the point—raising the issue is. Many teams will have a separate meeting after the Scrum (sometimes referred to as the "parking lot," as in "Let's take this out to the parking lot afterward") to delve into and resolve these issues.

Sprint Review

Duration: 4 hours
Participants: Full Scrum team

At the end of a sprint, the development team presents and demonstrates the potentially shippable product increment to the product owner and any interested stakeholders. The product owner goes through the product backlog items completed during the sprint. The development team then demonstrates each feature developed during the sprint and discusses what it learned in the implementation process that might impact other items.

The product owner puts the work accomplished in context, describing how the completion of the sprint fits into the overall product development and what backlog items remain.

All meeting participants may discuss any of these items, providing valuable feedback going into the next sprint planning meeting.

Sprint Retrospective

Duration: 3 hours
Participants: Full Scrum team

The sprint review is the opportunity for a team to demonstrate and discuss a product; the sprint retrospective provides the opportunity for the team to discuss the Scrum process itself.

Scrum isn't just about optimizing product development; it's also about continuously adjusting the *process* of development. During the retrospective, the team may discuss how the sprint went. Was there friction within the team? With external stakeholders? Were there problems getting resources or encountering roadblocks outside the team's control?

The Scrum master comes to the forefront during this meeting, providing expertise to help the team make improvements before the next sprint. The master may also resolve issues with outsiders. In his capacity as supreme yogi and troubleshooter, the scrum master can deploy his superior agile knowledge to help either the team or organization better deliver value to the customer in the form of working software.

Positive feedback should also feature in the retrospective. The Scrum master should ensure that what went right receives equal time with what went wrong. Reinforcing what the team is doing well is just as important as identifying what can be done better.

Scrum Framework

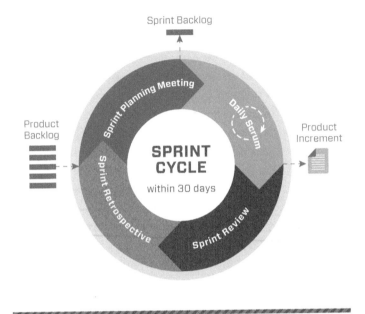

The Scrum Team

PRODUCT OWNER

- Owns the product backlog and prioritizes items

- Acts as interface between Scrum team and external stakeholders

- Makes final judgment on whether a product is a potentially viable shippable product increment

SCRUM MASTER

- Has mastered agile principles and Scrum

- Serves as a resource for both the product owner and development team

- Helps improve Scrum team

- Facilitates communication among team and with external stakeholders

DEVELOPMENT TEAM

- Works as a self-organized, unified group

- Creates item estimates

- Completes product backlog items to agreed-upon standards

Figure 1: A visual representation of a 30-day Scrum cycle.

Helpful Scrum Tools, Practices, and Concepts

By now, you've read about the "official" Scrum roles and artifacts. But few teams practice Scrum in such an austere fashion. Over the years, a number of complementary practices and techniques have emerged that enhance and improve Scrum and have become almost as closely identified with the framework as the basic components themselves.

Feel the Burn

Foremost among these extra artifacts is the venerable burn-down chart, which plots work completed over time (see figure 2 on page 60). The units of measure depend on what the team is comfortable working with, whether that's dollars, story points, hours, or days. Some teams prefer to burn up instead of burn down; if this is your preference, look at the burn-down chart upside down and backward.

Burn charts add transparency to the development process. Usually, they're posted in a common area of the site and available to anyone involved with the project.

Frequently, you plot burn charts using two lines. One is the initial, ideal estimate of task completion over time, predicting how many tasks should remain at any given interval. The second is the actual progression, typically less straightforward and showing the tasks remaining at each point.

The actual progression might also occasionally jump in the wrong direction, as hands-on work reveals unanticipated tasks required to complete an item. This isn't unusual, unexpected, or even unfortunate; revealing problems as early as possible is part of the Scrum ethos. It lets teams adjust to the reality of complex development instead of proceeding obliviously in accordance with a plan that has become outdated.

A quick comparison of the lines on the chart lets everyone on the team visualize progress both in terms of tasks completed and tasks remaining. Over the long term, burn-down charts can help a team adjust velocity and make more accurate predictions for future sprints.

While sprint-specific burn-down charts are the most common, product owners also create burn-down charts that measure project progress from sprint to sprint.

Project X Burn-Down Chart

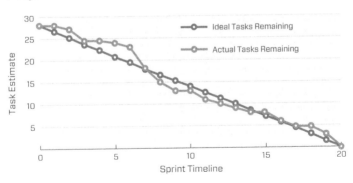

Figure 2: A basic burn-down chart.

Please Release Me

Products are made to be used, but Scrum doesn't say anything about when you should release them. Sure, at the end of each sprint you had better have a PSPI, but that's not to say it's a truly shippable product. That, ultimately, is a business decision.

Many businesses apply agile management to the development process but not to the release pipeline (although recent trends, such as DevOps and Agile Operations, are beginning to shift operations and deployment functions in some organizations in a more agile direction). Some products simply can't be built in their entirety in the span of a single sprint.

At the other end of the spectrum, some companies practice continuous deployment, where they release items to customers as soon as they complete them—even if that happens before the natural end of the sprint.

Whatever the reason, release planning is a matter of concern for product owners and stakeholders.

Full product releases will inevitably run into the so-called Iron Triangle of project-management constraints: scope, resources, and schedule. Adjusting any of these constraints can affect the others. For example, adding features to the scope typically requires either more resources (software developers) or more time to implement.

Since you can't predict project roadblocks, it's a virtual certainty that some combination of scope, resources, and schedule will change over the course of a project. In Scrum projects that use a single team, the resources—the development team—are fixed. The team can only accomplish so much in any given sprint. As a result, you can only adjust a project's scope and schedule.

Alas, for legitimate business reasons, you might find either of those constraints fixed, too. For example, tax software might have to be released before a fixed filing deadline, creating a scheduling constraint. Or it might need a capital gains calculator for the product to have any value to customers, which is a scope issue.

The trade-offs required to meet the constraints may be difficult, but they're common business decisions. The difficulty with Scrum is predicting where conflicts will arise on a long enough horizon to reconcile the release plan. Because the framework explicitly calls for less detailed planning for lower-priority items, it can be hard to visualize what the product will look like near the project's end.

To resolve this, the product owner can engage in meta-planning outside the Scrum framework. Although only the development team can ultimately decide how many items to take on in a given sprint, the product owner will have some idea of what the team can accomplish from its velocity. He can then roughly map features onto upcoming sprints to try to predict the feature sets the team can finish by specific dates.

Although teams can't accurately estimate low-priority items near the beginning of a project, this mapping exercise might help the product owner group items into feature sets that produce the best incremental product in naturally releasable segments.

Scoped Out

In a properly run Scrum framework, there's no such thing as scope creep—or, if there is, it's for good reason, like changing business priorities or marketplace realities. Scrum is designed to let product owners adjust scope mid-project as a way of adapting to new information or altered market conditions.

But not all Scrum teams are well run, and there's enough slack in the iterative sprint cycle for weak-willed product owners to slip into scope creep.

The Scrum framework itself doesn't offer a solution. In fact, the ability of only a product owner to change backlog item priorities is a *feature* of the system. This is an instance where the Scrum master might step in to counsel the owner, or reach out to management outside the team for an intervention. Close cooperation between the product owner and outside stake-holders can also help limit the potential for creep.

> Scope creep is an ancient problem for software projects, particularly long-running and preplanned projects. If requirements and capabilities are mismatched, or if an extended period of time passes between the product definition and implementation, the development team can find itself shooting at a constantly moving target. The customer keeps coming back and asking for some-thing just a tiny bit different from the original spec. And then they do it again. And again. And again.

High Speed, Low Drag

You can tell a team's velocity from its burn-down chart, which simply graphs the amount of work done in a sprint.

A lot of teams put too much weight on velocity. In truth, no metric other than increments of potentially shippable software is a definitive measure of a team's performance. But because velocity is easy to calculate and serves as a proxy for efficiency, many teams are judged based on it.

Most teams find that velocity increases naturally over time as individual members improve their performance and cross-train one another to get more done in a fixed amount of time. But at some point, velocity will hit a plateau.

When that happens, the best way to improve velocity is to improve the Scrum process itself. A good Scrum master is invaluable at this stage. They can suggest internal organizational hacks to increase team efficiency, or analyze impediments external to the team that may slow progress. With their special standing, the Scrum master should seek to work with the team and others in the company to clear obstacles and boost velocity.

Tell Me a Story

Agility stresses interaction between developers and customers (as well as among developers), but communication isn't as easy as just having a chat. Most users don't speak geek. They have problems they want solved and things they want accomplished, but they don't have the vocabulary to express them in technical terms. The very process of discussing software with developers can be intimidating for nontechnical users. As a result, many Scrum teams use a more familiar format to produce understandable item requirements: story time.

During story time, a customer (or customer proxy; the product owner often fills this role) is encouraged to tell, in plain English, a simple story about what they want to accomplish. It may start out something like this: "As a website user, I want to be able to add an item to my shopping cart so I can continue shopping before buying it."

Users are encouraged to keep their stories brief. Everything should fit on a 3x5 card or sticky note. This doesn't mean they can't describe big features. "As a website user, I want to shop for the finest gourmet dog foods on the market for my beloved pooch" is a perfectly valid user story of the sort often called an *epic*. Epics are stories too big to implement in a single sprint. There is also often the implication that they represent sets of functions that would represent little value if developed independently of one another. For Scrum purposes, epics must be broken down into smaller component stories that software developers can develop in a single sprint. For example, developers might separate the dog food story into stories such as "As a website user I want to see a grid of pictures and descriptions of dog foods for sale" and "As a website user I want to be able to click a button to add a bag of dog food to my cart for eventual purchase." But it's clear that neither of those stories represents much value without the other.

Breaking down epics into user stories of an appropriate size to develop in a single sprint is part of backlog grooming. Although not all stories belonging to a given epic might fit in one sprint, they will usually be scheduled in adjacent sprints so that the epic can be realized in as short a time frame as possible.

Deal Me In

Group dynamics can make estimating product backlog item sizes difficult for many teams. Groupthink can develop around the first estimation uttered, leading to inaccurate estimates.

Planning Poker has developed as a fun way to avoid this possibility and inject a little entertainment into the otherwise dry process of size estimation. The team plays the game with real cards, although not the standard 52-card deck. Instead, each player gets a deck of Planning Poker cards. It contains somewhere between 6 and 13 cards, numbered in a modified Fibonacci sequence—this assumes that developers estimate items in arbitrary story points, although individual teams are free to make estimates in whatever denomination they agree on. Some sets have a card marked with the drawing of a coffee cup or the symbol for pi, indicating "Hey, I'm tired and need some pie and coffee, it's time to take a break." Many also have a question mark, indicating, "I have no earthly idea how to estimate the size of this item."

The product owner presents the item the team needs to estimate, and the usual clarification process occurs, with development team members asking questions until they understand the item. Then each of them privately selects a

Project X Story Map

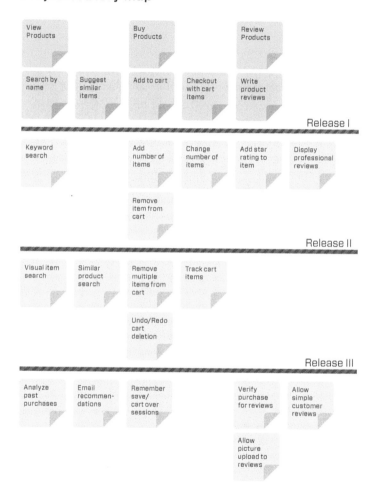

Figure 3: A basic story map of the different groups of user stories required to develop a hypothetical e-commerce website.

card representing the value they believe the item should be estimated at. They simultaneously play their cards, revealing the estimate.

If all the cards are identical, that's the estimate for the item. In the more likely case where they differ, a discussion ensues. The team members who differ—usually starting with the player of the high card and then the player of the low card—describe the reasoning behind their estimates to expose any mistaken assumptions or differences in opinion.

After this, the team continues to play rounds of Planning Poker until the members reach a consensus for each item. The Scrum master acts as a sort of "dealer" in the game, facilitating the discussion to ensure the team reaches genuine consensus.

Planning Poker

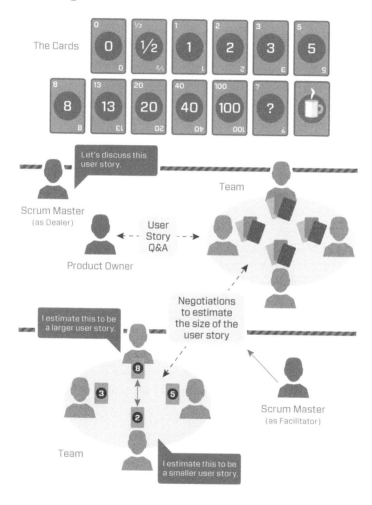

Figure 4: Planning poker in action.

ABNORMAL TERMINATION

No Scrum team wants to hear the phrase *abnormal termination*. It's the act of aborting a sprint before it's done.

That can happen for a variety of reasons. Happily, relatively few have to do with the Scrum team. As rare as abnormal terminations are, they're even more rarely due to some flaw or misstep on the part of the team. Typically, external forces cause them: a competing product introduces a radical new concept that your own project must address, your company runs out of money, or an international zombie plague breaks out . . . that sort of thing.

When this happens, you don't just switch off your computer and walk away (unless it's the zombie thing). Instead, stop work but continue the normal Scrum cycle: hold a sprint review to demonstrate any items completed during the sprint, and discuss the product direction in light of the termination.

You'll especially want to hold a sprint retrospective for the team. An abnormal termination can be disconcerting. How the team handles it can tell you a lot about how they adapt to the Scrum process. The Scrum master can provide important guidance and improve the understanding of why the sprint was terminated and how the team can best proceed.

3 SCRUM IN ACTION

Adapted and Agile

So now you understand Scrum. You're in your assigned role, you know your responsibilities, and you got a good night's sleep and a fresh cup of coffee. You're ready to start putting together the artifacts. And that's when things will begin to go wrong.

Don't panic! In Scrum, there's no stigma associated with errors. The entire point of the framework is to identify and correct problems calmly and systematically. When you run into that first big problem, congratulations! You didn't screw up—you just had your first Scrum success. Now you've got something to talk about at the Daily Scrum!

A Sprint in the Life of a Scrum Team

Every Scrum team, even among teams within the same company, is different. Part of the point of Scrum is to adapt so that individuals can accomplish tasks in the most efficient way they know how. Every team's sprint is a little different.

The sprint planning meeting kicks off every sprint. The entire Scrum team gathers so the product owner can present the highest-priority items from the product backlog. The list probably represents an amount of estimated work roughly in line with what the team accomplished during previous sprints. Still, there will likely be some discussion of each item to ensure that everyone understands it completely and that the development team unanimously agrees on which items to include on the current sprint backlog.

During the second half of the meeting, the product owner takes a back seat. The development team decides, among themselves, how to break the items down into programming tasks. If a question comes up about what constitutes done or about the item itself, the development team may consult the product owner to clarify. If an issue bogs down the process, the Scrum master can step in to help facilitate an agreement.

With the sprint backlog in hand, the development team gets to work. The rest of their day will be like most days of the sprint: work, interspersed with as few process-related impediments as possible.

First among the process events is usually the Daily Scrum. The team huddles up, and each member addresses three items: what they accomplished since the last Daily Scrum, what they plan to accomplish before the next one, and what obstacles

The Scrum master doesn't have very many explicit tasks during the average sprint. You might think that, because they aren't mentioned much in sprint discussions, they don't have much to do. In fact, Scrum masters should be active all the time—reviewing the Scrum process, evaluating it, suggesting tips and improvements, and nudging the team in the right direction.

they believe may impede them. Everyone stands; no one is allowed to talk about anything other than these three items. The Scrum master may apply a freshly cut birch switch to enforce these rules.

If further discussion is necessary, a series of smaller follow-up meetings may be held to remove obstacles or address questions any team member has about another's report.

Then it's just work. Usually, the development team sits together in a single room, or at least in the same part of the building. Scrum emphasizes interaction and cooperative work. Where you might have turned immediately to the Internet to solve a problem in other jobs, you'll now probably turn to a teammate first.

You'll make adjustments throughout the sprint. Chances are, you won't end up working on what you thought you would when you first built the sprint backlog. Tasks will be adjusted and shuffled around. Every day, you'll reevaluate where you are and keep everyone in the loop. You might drop or pick up tasks or items depending on your progress and that of the rest of the team. The Scrum master may be involved, helping you work around problems or talking through better ways to approach them.

From time to time during the week, the development team will probably change things up a bit by sitting down with the product owner to evaluate and discuss items from the product backlog. And, at the end of the sprint, you'll host the sprint review, where you present the current product and the sprint retrospective, discussing what went right and wrong during the sprint.

Top Ten

Knowing Scrum team roles and understanding project
artifacts and activities is important, but some people may
still find it challenging to adapt to an agile environment. It
can be radically different from traditional offices, and people
are uncomfortable with change, even when it's for the better.
And it's not always really better—adjustments to Scrum can
legitimately diminish aspects of pride and enjoyment that
certain people have invested in their waterfall roles, even as
the overall process and efficiency of the organization improve.
Good managers should recognize this and make adjustments
accordingly.

1. **Be sure Scrum is what you need.** Scrum isn't the only agile
   framework around, and agile isn't the only development
   method out there. Neither is a universal solution. Make
   sure you have the right framework for your organization.

2. **Acknowledge organizational discomfort.** Transitioning
   to Scrum isn't natural or easy for everyone; be empathetic
   to and accommodating of staff members who have problems with the framework.

3. **Don't scrimp on your Scrum master.** The role can be ill-
   defined enough that management doesn't want to hire a
   Scrum master for each new Scrum project. They try to
   combine the role with one of the others on the Scrum team
   or remove it entirely. Don't let this happen! Leaving out the
   person who knows the most about the framework just as
   you adopt it is a sure way to get things wrong.

4. **Start with culture, not tools.** Scrum is a popular agile framework, but it's just a tool. A *process*. The Agile Manifesto spells this out for you: *individuals and interactions over processes and tools*. The culture of your organization—how individuals interact with one another—will ultimately determine the success of your Scrum implementation.

5. **Don't get caught up in gimmicks.** Scrum artifacts and activities, and the practices associated with them, are great. But they can distract you as well. Don't lose track of agile principles in favor of obsessing over your burn-down numbers. Interaction, acceptance of change, and working software must be your focus.

6. **Focus on the agile principles.** If you have an apparent conflict between a Scrum practice and the Agile Manifesto, the choice is easy: stick with the underlying principle.

7. **Do the hard parts.** It's inevitable that, at some stage of your Scrum implementation, you're going to find it hard to meet some requirement or another. Maybe you can't get everyone together for a sprint review. Maybe you can't break a user story down to fit into a single sprint. And someone will say, "Well, let's just skip that this time." *Don't do it*. At some point, you'll learn to tinker with the process successfully. But when you're starting out, maintain discipline.

8. **Sit together.** Scrum doesn't explicitly require that teams be co-located, but most successful Scrum projects involve putting the team in the same room.

9. **Don't forget the outside world.** At the end of the day, your product is going somewhere else, either inside or outside your organization. Chances are, *agile* is a foreign term there. Think about how your team will work with outside dependents or dependencies that don't use agile principles.

10. **Have fun.** Sustainability is an agile principle that sometimes gets lost in the sprint mentality. Make sure you don't lose your verve for getting up and going to work in the morning.

Case Studies

Microsoft Developer Division

Organization: Microsoft Corp., Developer Division

Product: Development tool sets, including Visual Studio and Visual Studio Online

Background: Of all the possible validations for the Scrum framework, its adoption by the company that was responsible for producing most of the software that all other software runs on has to be the biggest.

A few development teams at Microsoft practiced various agile methods almost from agile's inception. But transitioning the Developer Division to agile introduced the framework to the holiest of holies—the people who made the software tools that created the company's code were being given a new tool for making the tools. Talk about iteration!

Some of the software giant's most experienced software developers worked in the Developer Division. Yet the pressure of adapting to cloud-based services and other changing technologies affected them as much as the rest of the company. The pressure to develop and deliver new software features and toolsets more rapidly became an impediment to using the traditional two-year waterfall development lifecycle.

Implementation: With around 500 employees in the Developer Division, Microsoft couldn't adopt Scrum overnight. In fact, bringing Scrum into the division was a three-year journey. Every employee, starting with upper management, went through Scrum training. Corporate buy-in was a necessity and a priority. Simply building the initial product backlog was a major undertaking.

Microsoft made both physical and psychological changes. It remodeled Building 18, home of the programming division, ripping out individual offices—a Microsoft hallmark—and replacing them with team rooms.

The division settled on a three-week sprint cycle as standard. It assembled cross-functional teams without changing the company's organizational structure. Instead, each team was composed of a subteam of individuals from the Project Management, Development, and Quality Assurance groups, still managed by their existing leads. They stayed together for 12 to 18 months.

The size of the project and the organization introduced other strains on Scrum standards. Sprint review meetings, for example, were an obstacle. Getting every stakeholder to attend a product demonstration every three weeks would have been a logistical nightmare. Instead, product owners produced videos demonstrating the features and emailed the videos to stakeholders. The stakeholders could then review and comment, or they could ask questions in their own time.

Because agile calls for face-to-face communication, Microsoft also brought together teams and managers every third sprint.

These sorts of adaptation are the name of the game for Scrum in the Developer Division. It ignores traditional metrics like burn-down, velocity, estimates, and capacity. It doesn't necessarily finish features in a single sprint. Development may overlap. The primary goal is to let the engineering team remain flexible, not to rigidly adhere to the Scrum framework. Scrum masters often simultaneously fill other roles on the team.

In this sense, Microsoft is a clear example of practicing ScrumBut. Nonetheless, the Developer Division now delivers more frequently, with fewer defects, and is more responsive to customer feedback—an agile win regardless of what you choose to call it.

Adobe Premiere Pro

Organization: Adobe

Product: Premiere Pro

Background: Premiere Pro is video-editing software first released by Adobe in 2003. It competes with the more popular Avid Media Composer and Apple Final Cut Pro. Premiere Pro was handicapped by running only on Windows machines in an industry that is almost exclusively based on Macs, so in 2005 the Premiere Pro team launched a two-year "Back to the Mac" effort to port the software.

The team spent six months in bug-fix mode, which became such a death march that some developers ended up in the hospital with exhaustion from overwork.

Despite the effort, the release wasn't a screaming success. The team contrasted their experiences with those of another product team, Soundbooth, which had already adopted Scrum. The Soundbooth team released its product with a low defect count, low stress, and high quality and stability.

After attending a training session conducted by Scrum co-creator Ken Schwaber, the Adobe video group leadership team decided to transition the entire group to agile development.

Implementation: Using internal resources, the Premiere Pro team underwent two days of Scrum training and then began collaborating on the initial product backlog. It split into three cross-functional Scrum teams, each sharing a single Scrum master and product owner.

The product owner was backed by a collaborative Product Owner Council composed of other stakeholders in the organization. Although the entire council could comment on the project and assist the product owner with his responsibilities, only the designated owner had the final say.

Difficulties with the teams surfaced quickly. The cross-functional development teams had been assembled without respect to location, and some who were geographically remote had difficulty connecting with their teammates. And developers who had long been accustomed to approaching engineering problems with layered solutions—first build the storage system, then the data access layer, then the business logic—had difficulty envisioning architecture developed in thin vertical slices around individual user stories. Finally, the team had dependencies on other internal product teams that had *not* adopted agile methods. Their releases weren't in sync.

But the team met each challenge in stride. It used video conferencing and collaboration tools—already an Adobe specialty—to integrate geographically remote teams. Developers learned to build in vertical slices around features simply by digging in and experimenting. And internal evangelists worked with non-agile teams to help them become more iterative and alter their release system to better accommodate the agile teams.

By the time Adobe released the next version of Premiere Pro, internal surveys of the team showed a marked increase in confidence in the product. The peak internal defect rate was 43 percent lower than the previous release. Eighty percent of the team was sold on continuing with Scrum. No one ended up in the hospital.

The business outcome was positive as well. The new version jumped in customer satisfaction surveys, taking a lead over Final Cut Pro and narrowing the gap with the industry-leading Media Composer.

FBI Sentinel

Organization: Federal Bureau of Investigation

Product: Sentinel Case Management System

Background: The federal government came to the information technology revolution late—as recently as 2003, the FBI kept most of its records on paper. It conceived a new electronic case file management system, called Sentinel, to digitize these records and automate their handling, giving agents around the world immediate access and vastly improving their ability to search and compare information from investigations.

The bureau began using the new system in 2006, using conventional phase-driven development implemented by an outside contractor. By 2010, the FBI had invested more than $400 million, but less than half the system had been developed.

Implementation: In mid-2010, the FBI fired the contractor, and the bureau's CTO assembled an in-house team to take over coding. The development team shrank from the contractor's 400-plus people to an in-house team of 45 working out of the FBI's basement. Only 15 of the 45 were software developers.

The new team was not only smaller, it committed to delivering the software faster. Using Scrum, the team adopted a two-week sprint cycle. It identified almost 700 user stories and mapped them to each of the functional requirements in the original system specification. Although more than half of the software's functions remained to be delivered, the plan called for the project to be done by September 2011.

By the end of that year, the team had finished only half of the software's feature set. An incomplete definition of done resulted in some story items requiring redevelopment after they had supposedly been completed. Worse, a pilot release to FBI field offices in October 2011 revealed that the hardware available was insufficient to meet the software's demands. Two systemwide crashes resulted.

But the benefits of the Scrum approach were evident. Although issues had been uncovered and the delivery date pushed back, the project remained well within budget. It was finally deployed systemwide in July 2012.

Scrum has run into other problems in government service. The agile emphasis on minimal documentation sometimes doesn't sit well with the paper-pushers. In particular, security personnel felt that the final system wasn't sufficiently documented for them to fulfill various compliance requirements. And the lack of a formal staffing plan left the inspector general's office aflutter with concerns that "managers are unable to make fully informed and effective staffing decisions."

But the inspector general's report also lauded the agile approach for reducing the risk of development. Although problems occurred in the Scrum process, they had been quickly identified and resolved. The FBI credited the agile approach with salvaging a project that had been mired in uncertainty.

Anonymous

Organization: Anonymous

Product: Internal Data Catalog Project

Background: As much as agile approaches represent a categorically improved process for software projects, Scrum projects can still fail.

Understandably, few organizations or Scrum professionals are comfortable talking about those failures, and when they do so, they generally choose to remain anonymous, as does the subject of this case study.

The organization in question had an organic internal data collection system composed of a manually populated spread-sheet that flowed into a custom Java application, which, in turn, fed a variety of other systems. The company elected to replace the system with a customized implementation of a commercial software package.

Implementation: The company selected Scrum as the project-management methodology to handle installing the package and customizing the process. It assembled a strong internal team of a product owner intimately familiar with the existing data system and a number of experienced development team members. It brought in a number of experts from an outside consulting firm that specialized in modifying commercial software and an experienced Scrum master who had previously worked at the company and who knew some members of the team.

Problems began almost immediately. Two contractor-provided outside development team members turned out to have little experience with the product in question. Worse, the product owner proved to be invested in the existing system and saw no reason to replace it. The project was driven by managers outside the business unit that had created and relied on the system. There was no clear communication between that unit and downstream stakeholders who found the system inefficient—the business silos did not have clear agreement on the requirements for a replacement system.

The company replaced the product owner and added another inexperienced team member as initial releases proved unsatisfactory to a small group of pilot users.

The team began running into various organizational obstacles to development; IT department controls generated overhead that slowed progress and drove the team to adopt a completely separate development environment instead of the more realistic production system. Future product increments were reviewed internally rather than deployed to the pilot test group.

The new team member, from the IT department, began to act as a sort of information funnel, blocking interaction between the team and stakeholders and attempting to overlay a schedule on the development process—effectively implementing a phased system over the sprints.

The company took steps to blunt the influence of the new team member, but other external stakeholders apparently smelled blood in the water and began similarly circumventing the product owner to manipulate the team's direction.

Meanwhile, subsequent iterations continued to under-whelm users. Ultimately, the business pulled members off the Scrum team and quietly scaled the project down until it finally cancelled the project and abandoned a formal product release.

Intel Processor Testing

Organization: Intel

Product: Oregon and Pacific Product Development Engineering (PDE) team

Background: Most software developers write programs that run on Intel processors. The Intel PDE team creates a test framework to evaluate those microprocessors before they come to market.

The business unit, with about 50 employees, had a history of long death marches, missed deadlines, and scope creep, which led to low morale and high turnover. The manufacturing process at Intel drives the corporate culture, which is deeply engaged in traditional phased waterfall development. Intel plans its products years ahead of production and hands each sequential development step from one functional team to the next. Those teams weren't cross-functional, placing a signif-icant burden on domain experts within them when they were unable to distribute tasks.

Implementation: The team elected to implement Scrum to cure these various ills. During a down cycle between products, they brought in Scrum consultants and reorganized the group into six teams. By adopting the framework during a period of relatively low activity, the company hoped employees could learn and evaluate the process well enough to function at a high level during more critical stages of development.

Crucially, the Intel teams adopted Scrum "by the book" for their first pass at the framework. They didn't allow any existing organizational inertia to force them into shortcuts. Only after they had practiced the model for three months did they attempt to adapt it to their own business requirements.

The team couldn't get organizational buy-in to fund the Scrum master position, so it used volunteer Scrum masters. It ended up with three masters to mentor what became, by the end of the first three months, eight Scrum teams.

Within a year, those eight teams had become twelve. Given what they had learned during the pilot period, the team also added a number of functional roles not found in the vanilla Scrum framework. It split the product owner role into parts to allow better business oversight as well as more detailed technical ownership of particular features. The team also established a "transient" position to allow highly specialized domain experts to move between teams when their expertise was required on various sprints.

These roles helped Scrum fit better within the overall organization and let the group scale work more successfully across the Scrum teams.

By the time product development popped into high gear, the unit was ready to adapt. Most of the Scrum teams found themselves moving from two-week sprints to *one-day* sprints to accommodate the activity. The various associated meetings all collapsed into one morning meeting.

Although the pace was grueling, the discipline the teams learned and embraced during the pilot process paid off. Agile values and adaptability kept them effective and relaxed. After the demand waned, the teams went back to the conventional two-week sprints.

Today, the group has 18 Scrum teams, improved morale, increased transparency, and fewer defects and schedule slips than ever.

FAQ and Final Thoughts

When is it appropriate to use Scrum, and when should we look to other methodologies?

First, Scrum (or any new methodology) isn't going to work in organizations where the culture doesn't allow it. If you can't change the culture, there's no point in adopting Scrum.

Second, highly predictable or reliable products might not be a good fit for Scrum.

Finally, in any situation in which, for valid organizational or product constraints, a team can't follow the Scrum rules, it's probably not a good choice. For example, you might not be able to assemble a single cross-functional team that can genuinely, independently produce a potentially shippable product increment. Scrum has been adapted to such scenarios, but it's not ideal or recommended for beginners.

How does Scrum handle deadlines?

Deadlines are a business reality. Scrum has plenty of them, but it has nothing to say about final product release deadlines. You have to examine and resolve such requirements at the business level. Scrum might not be appropriate for products with fixed features and release dates.

On the other hand, some common assumptions about requirements are often simply obscured in waterfall systems; just because the plan calls for feature X to be done by date Y doesn't mean it will be done. Management has to weigh its certainty about deadlines against Scrum's risk reduction.

How does Scrum handle bad actors on the team?

Scrum has nothing to say about how companies allocate staff to a team; management has to remove incompetent or unsuitable staffers.

However, Scrum works to build teams, not tear them apart. Peer pressure and the dynamics of self-organization tend to bring people into line, and the Scrum master is responsible for coaching members (collectively and individually) on contributing meaningfully to a project.

How can Scrum prevent micromanagement?

If an organization has bad managers, no development method in the world will save a project. But Scrum provides a model that teams can use as a defense against meddling. Every description ever made of the framework asserts the importance of maintaining team integrity and allowing self-organization and self-determination through a project. If presenting that evidence to management doesn't help, nothing will.

How does Scrum handle product deployment or production hand-off to non-agile teams?

Organizations frequently encounter problems between software development and deployment. Although Scrum enables development teams to rapidly produce software of value to customers, operations and production teams don't usually have the means to actually deliver increments so quickly.

This is slowly changing as operational teams incorporate agile methods. DevOps is a new trend seeking to blend development and operations concerns, and bring agile principles into the operational realm. "Selling" Scrum isn't isolated to only the development group; the entire organization has to see the benefits of agile approaches.

How can we build a solid architecture without up-front planning?

Scrum frequently fails in design. Because it intentionally avoids specifying engineering practices, some teams disregard this aspect of product development. But just because design isn't mentioned doesn't make it unimportant—Scrum doesn't explicitly mention using computers for development either, but everyone on your development team has one, don't they?

Part of the answer is learning to build in discrete vertical blocks, as the Adobe Premiere team did, rather than relying on horizontal layers. And part of it is truly embracing the iterative approach, to allow architecture to emerge as the design requirements evolve.

What happens when the project is too large to complete with a single Scrum team in a reasonable amount of time?

There are a lot of ways to combine multiple Scrum teams to complete a large project; you can find some in the case studies above. But a more popular technique is known as a Scrum of Scrums, which uses a meta-Scrum approach to manage an overarching project while breaking the component teams into individual Scrums of ordinary (seven- to nine-person) team size.

On Failure

Newcomers to agile sometimes seem to think of it as magic pixie dust you can scatter on a project to make it succeed. But the data suggest otherwise. A 2011 study from *Dr. Dobb's Journal* found that agile projects only beat waterfall projects by around 10 percent on overall success rates. Ten percent is nothing to sneeze at, but it's not a revolution.

Scrum can help make some projects that might otherwise have failed successes, but victory isn't really the point. Agile's real magic is letting failing projects fail *fast*. Failing fast shows you the grim truth. You can act to correct the failures or you can cut your losses early, before that small failure turns into a big, expensive one. Agile reduces risk, but only if you acknowledge it. Scrum's pattern repetition can mask signs of failure, particularly within the team itself. There's always a temptation to give a shaky project just one more sprint to see if the team can pull it out of the fire at the next iteration.

Scrum doesn't allow for micromanagement, but it does require business managers who use the information the process exposes to make good business decisions.

Does Scrum fail? Many proponents claim there's no such thing as a failed Scrum project; any failure can be attributed to improper implementation, a position that's at once inarguable and unhelpful.

Another way to ask the question might be, "If Scrum can't fail, doesn't that make it the only rational choice for a product development framework?" Fewer people would agree with that statement.

Even some of the original signatories of the Agile Manifesto have become dissatisfied with how agile has evolved. Scrum co-founder Ken Schwaber estimates that some three-quarters of organizations adopting Scrum never realize the benefits they had hoped for. Andy Hunt, another signatory and co-author of *The Pragmatic Programmer*, believes that the term *agile* has become meaningless, devolving as it has into a jingoistic exercise in zealotry and self-promotion.

In fact, we're still trying to understand the complexities of technology development. Adaptability will be necessary outside the scope of the framework in years to come.

Agile probably doesn't represent the end of the road in development methodologies, either. Although adopting agile methods has vastly improved most aspects of software development, current agile techniques have shown some limitations. At least one recent study appears to show that some combination of agile and waterfall techniques might work best for large projects or where security is a concern.

It may be inevitable that any moderately successful business practice will attract opportunists and snake-oil salesmen. Businesses that jump on the bandwagon without fully understanding or implementing the methods will be seen as emblematic of the framework.

These aren't reasons to devalue the core concepts of either agile or Scrum. It's clear, though, that agile is no place for amateurs or dilettantes. Being able to inspect and adapt adequately requires knowledge and experience as well as flexibility.

GLOSSARY

Acceptance test: A set of criteria specified by the product owner, usually in coordination with external stakeholders, designed to assess whether a user story has been completed to the required standard.

Activity: A prescribed Scrum process described by the framework, or an ancillary practice used in concert with the official processes to assist with organizational or situational adaptation to Scrum.

Artifact: One of the prescribed Scrum lists (such as the product backlog) or objects (such as the potentially releasable product increment) described by the framework.

Burn-down chart: A two-axis graph plotting the amount of work estimated or completed against an interval of time (usually days or sprints).

Cross-functional: The quality of possessing all necessary skills required to function autonomously to complete required tasks.

Daily Scrum: A quick (15-minute maximum) meeting that takes place each day of a sprint. Participants remain standing and briefly state their status. Attended by, and used to coordinate among, the development team.

Development team: A group of self-organizing and cross-functional professionals who execute the work necessary to express the results of the items from the product backlog.

Epic: Common term used to refer to a very large user story from the product backlog, not yet broken down into pieces suitable for inclusion on a sprint backlog.

Estimate: An approximate calculation of the amount of work required to complete a product backlog item. The value might be stated in terms of days or hours of work, or in an arbitrary, relative scale called "story points."

Feature: An element of a product representing a function of value to the user.

Forecast: Alternative term for *commitment*, used to describe the items that make up the goal for a sprint.

Grooming: The process of developing, sizing, refining, and prioritizing product backlog items.

Ideal day/hour: An estimating term used to describe the size of product backlog items; the value is presumed to describe the amount of effort a task would take if all development time during a single day (or hour) were devoted to completing it.

Minimum viable product: The minimum set of features required to make a product viable for release to market.

Planning Poker: A game designed to help produce unbiased product estimates.

Potentially shippable product increment (PSPI): The realization of the work completed in a sprint, the precise dimensions of which the Scrum team defines.

Product backlog: The cumulative list of items describing features that, if completed, would accurately describe the completed product under development.

Product backlog item: A single item (often referred to as a user story) on the product backlog. The item concisely describes a feature and includes a size estimate, value, and priority.

Product owner: The single person responsible for the expression of the ultimate design and delivery of the product via ownership of the product backlog.

Scrum master: A facilitator, coach, and resource attached to a Scrum team to lend expertise and assistance at implementing Scrum and removing impediments to development.

Self-organizing: A theory of management that delegates authority to the employees closest to and most familiar with the job tasks at hand. Collaboration and peer coordination are used to arrive at a consensus management effort.

Sprint: A single time-boxed iteration of one month or less, during which the development team attempts to implement the items on the current sprint backlog.

Sprint backlog: A subset of the product backlog items that a team will work on and implement during the current sprint. It is the product of a sprint planning meeting.

Sprint backlog item: A single item, or user story, from the product backlog that has been moved to the sprint backlog. Once on the sprint backlog, the item becomes "locked" from modification by any person outside the development team.

Sprint goal: A high-level overview of the tasks that the product owner hopes the development team will accomplish during the current sprint in broad terms of overall product functionality.

Sprint planning: The process of creating a sprint backlog from product backlog items and deciding how to best complete those items during the upcoming sprint.

Sprint retrospective: A meeting of the Scrum team to review how the Scrum process performed during the most recent sprint.

Sprint review: A brief meeting demonstrating the potentially releasable product increment created during the most recent sprint.

Stakeholder: A person or group outside the Scrum team with an interest in the product in development.

Story: *See* User story.

Story points: Arbitrary points affixed to product backlog items to represent the amount of work a story represents relative to other stories.

Task: An item of work, more discrete and time-bound than a story point, representing one of several work items that may be required to realize a product backlog item.

Test-driven development: A common technical practice on agile teams that relies on writing a failing (usually automated) test construct to evaluate the performance of a particular function before attempting to implement it.

Time-boxed: Constrained by time in some sense.

User story: A common format for the description of product backlog items. The general approach states the issue casually in the form of "As a [type of user], I want to be able to [complete a goal] in order to [create a type of value]."

Value: The importance or worth of a feature or product.

Velocity: A measure of work efficiency calculated by dividing work units by time units.

Waterfall: A broad description of sequential, linear development processes that cascade downward over time in discrete phases according to a previously established plan or blueprint.

RESOURCES

Agile Alliance
www.agilealliance.org
A nonprofit organization that supports agile practitioners and puts on an annual conference for practitioners of agile software development.

Scrum.org
www.scrum.org
Scrum co-founder Ken Schwaber's resource and tool site for Scrum practitioners.

Scrummasterchecklist.org
www.scrummasterchecklist.org
A handy checklist of considerations and tasks, valuable to experienced and novice Scrum masters alike.

Scrum Alliance
www.scrumalliance.org
The nonprofit organization that certifies and maintains standards for Scrum framework training.

BOOKS AND ARTICLES

Rubin, Kenneth S. *Essential Scrum: A Practical Guide to the Most Popular Agile Process.* Upper Saddle River, NJ: Addison-Wesley, 2013.
A comprehensive look at the Scrum framework, and a better overview of the ancillary adaptations required to flesh out the development process than most Scrum books offer.

Schwaber, Ken. *Agile Project Management with Scrum.* Redmond, WA: Microsoft Press, 2004.
An in-depth look at Scrum, with many practical examples, from the framework's co-creator.

Schwaber, Ken, and Jeff Sutherland. *The Scrum Guide.* Scrum.org, 2013.
The official "by the book" version of Scrum as penned by its two creators.

Sims, Chris, and Hillary Louise Johnson. *The Elements of Scrum.* Foster City, CA: Dymaxicon, 2011.
A brief, direct overview of the Scrum framework with quick descriptions of a number of popular ancillary processes.

Takeuchi, Hirotaka, and Ikujiro Nonaka. "The New New Product Development Game." *Harvard Business Review.* January 1986. Accessed June 2015. hbr.org/1986/01/the-new-new-product-development-game.
The article that started it all, analyzing modern lean development techniques with the scrum analogy of a rugby team pushing the project down the field in unison.

REFERENCES

Awad, M. A. "A Comparison between Agile and Traditional Software Development Methodologies." 2005. Accessed June 2015. www.unf .edu/~broggio/cen6940/ComparisonAgileTraditional.pdf.

Bjork, Aaron. "Scaling Agile across the Enterprise." Accessed June 2015. stories.visualstudio.com/scaling-agile-across-the-enterprise/ index.html.

Brooks, Frederick P. *The Mythical Man-Month: Essays on Software Engineering*. Rev. ed. Boston: Addison-Wesley, 1995.

Elwer, Pat. "Agile Project Development at Intel: A Scrum Odyssey." 2008. Accessed June 2015. www.danube.com/docs/case_studies/ Intel_case_study.pdf.

Green, Peter. "Adobe Premiere Pro Scrum Adoption: How an Agile Approach Enabled Success in a Hyper-Competitive Landscape." August 2015. Accessed June 2015. blogs.adobe.com/agile/ files/2012/08/Adobe-Premiere-Pro-Scrum-Adoption-How -an-agile-approach-enabled-success-in-a-hyper-competitive -landscape.pdf.

Hunt, Andrew, and David Thomas. *The Pragmatic Programmer: From Journeyman to Master*. Reading, MA: Addison-Wesley, 1999.

Lo Giudice, Diego, Holger Kisker, and Nasrey Angel. "How Can You Scale Your Agile Adoption? Results from Forrester's Q3 2013 Global Agile Software Application Development Online Survey." February 5, 2014. Accessed June 2015. www.forrester.com/ go?objectid=RES110444.

Mieritz, Lars. "Gartner Survey Shows Why Projects Fail." June 10, 2013. Accessed June 2015. www.thisiswhatgoodlookslike .com/2012/06/10/gartner-survey-shows-why-projects-fail.

Ries, Eric. *The Lean Startup: How Today's Entrepreneurs Use Continuous Innovation to Create Radically Successful Businesses.* New York: Crown Business, 2011.

Royce, Winston. R. "Managing the Development of Large Software Systems." In *Technical Papers of Western Electronic Show and Convention.* Los Angeles, 1970.

Rubin, Kenneth S. *Essential Scrum: A Practical Guide to the Most Popular Agile Process.* Upper Saddle River, NJ: Addison-Wesley, 2013.

Schwaber, Ken. *Agile Project Management with Scrum.* Redmond, WA: Microsoft Press, 2004.

Schwaber, Ken, and Jeff Sutherland. *The Scrum Guide.* Scrum.org, 2013.

Scrum.org. scrum.org.

Scrum Alliance. www.scrumalliance.org.

Sims, Chris, and Hillary Louise Johnson. *The Elements of Scrum.* Foster City, CA: Dymaxicon, 2011.

Suscheck, Charles. "The Origins and Future of Scrum: An Interview with Ken Schwaber." April 30, 2014. Accessed June 2015. www.agileconnection.com/interview/origins-and-future-scrum-interview-ken-schwaber.

Takeuchi, Hirotaka, and Ikujiro Nonaka. "The New New Product Development Game." *Harvard Business Review.* January 1986. Accessed June 2015. hbr.org/1986/01/the-new-new-product-development-game.

U.S. Department of Justice, Office of the Inspector General. "Status of the Federal Bureau of Investigations Implementation of the Sentinel Project." December 2011. Accessed June 2015. oig.justice.gov/reports/2011/a1208.pdf.

INDEX

CPSIA information can be obtained at www.ICGtesting.com
Printed in the USA
BVOW11s0750261215

431037BV00025B/147/P